Spiritual Poems

By
Charles Gadbois

About The Author

Back in the day, growing up in the early 1980s, I watched Billy Gram on a small 13-inch TV. With no channel changer. Starting out with spiritual values in a small town called Cleveland, Oklahoma. Through humble beginnings, being young and so carefree. I had 2 brothers, and we ended up moving to Bryan, Texas, in 1990.

My whole life, I have enjoyed drawing. Having a keen eye for detail. Throughout my life, I have spent a lot of time lifting weights at the gym. A small part of my life, back in 2002, I started riding motorcycles. I rode for 10 years and loved the taste of freedom. Through the open winds, there is nothing like it. I haven't ridden a motorcycle in 14 years.

Years later, in my 40s, I started writing poems through rhythms and melodies. I've stayed truly focused on writing poetry for 2 years. My first book, published on September 26, 2024, is called 100 Poems With Coffee. A year later, I published a second book called 200 Poems with Coffee, Part 2.

Soon after, my 3rd book with illustrations was released. Darkest Poems With Coffee. There are too many poems to choose from to be my favorite. I have spent a lot of time writing and typing away through endless hours.

Take time out to read each poem with coffee. Lay down your burdens and camp out through a spiritual journey. I'm just an old soul writing poetry.

Charles Gadbois

Table of Contents

2 Small Copper Coins

Under the sun, an old lady stood in line.
She had to wait her turn; she didn't mind.
She was alone with not much to say.
She was a poor widow that never complained.
In front of the line stood the rich, giving very little.
I like this verse because it was short and powerful.
When the old lady stood in front of the table.
All she had was 2 small copper coins to give as she was humble.
A small gift can go a long way.
After all this time, a powerful message was given in poverty.
When was the last time you offered a good deed?
Not to ask for anything in return through the treasury.
What a great example it was that she gave all she had in the collection box.
She walked away in abundance on the sidewalk.
Sometimes we need to take time out and to be humble.
Not to complain and to worry about tomorrow.
Through the horizon we are beyond blessed.
Give it all to Jesus, for he will give us rest.
The old lady in a short verse gave her all.
Embrace the moment through temperament and stand tall.
We are all unique in our own way.
I love the open wind after it rains.
Be the one who holds the lamp and shows the light.

You are the one so beautiful standing in white.
You showed me the way when I was down.
In loneliness you understood, and now I am found.

7/9

Luke 21:1-4

88 Keys

Bass, middle, treble range. Piano, favorite instrument.
Unique sound.
Array of strings abound.
Dust settles.
Million songs created.
88 keys.
Each sound is beautifully made.
Peddle travels volume.
A music maker.
230 strings.
Moonlight, playing
Settle and soothing.
Heart resting.
Tears falling.
Songs moving.
Dressed in black.
Sounds from a piano are magical.

12/16

343

A tragic event 23 years ago.
A picture can say 1,000 words.
In memory of those we lost.
Time has passed, we have not forgotten.
How could this happen?
Survive and move on.
343 and the brave.
In honor till this day.
A hijack in the sky.
Two planes crash in sight.
This will change our lives forever.
So many worked in the Twin Towers.
I just wanted to say thank you.
For our firefighters that day at our Nation Capital.
New York is home for many.
Stand with us while the terrorist bleeds.
Stand strong into tomorrow. Honor them in a memorial. (2006)
Never forget that morning.
Unite this country in new beginnings. Raise up our colors.
Red, white and blue for our brothers.

7/21

A Dying Plant

Feeding everyone lies
The drama never dies
Running away from the root of the problem
Too many excuses with no water
Always playing the victim under the sun
Falling away into a sinkhole
You had plenty of chances
To make good choices
You choose to rebel in dirt
A stubborn generation
You never listened A dying plant
A heart full of regret
An ungrateful flower
Just freeloaders
A dying plant
I gave you guidance
You did everything your way
Flowers are fading
Bondage is breaking
Blaming someone else is never-ending The root of the problem
is burning

5/15/25

A Great Friend

Walk with me in the shadows
Raise me up when I'm down
Everybody hurts
Hard times here and there
Soul drowning
Sometimes
Find me in the dark
A true friend at heart
Many miles apart
Life de-railed
Heart uncertain
You've always carried the lamp
A great friend to lean on
Sometimes everybody hurts
Pondering with a cup of coffee staring out the window
I just wanted to say thank you
Strive to improve
Melody through sweat whispers

8/14/25

A Peaceful Journey

Even though I'm growing older, it's OK.
The passion for writing poetry. Calm through melody.
Even if I'm running out of time,
Keep on documenting until my last day.
I won't be six feet under in a grave.
All be writing poems in the indigo sky.
A peaceful journey.
With two great kids.
All of my writings will be theirs.
For now, write with black-ink into tomorrow.
Through creative writings. Rhythms and rhymes.
Pen in hand is therapeutic.
I am a workaholic.
Always behind with my work.
Document your journey through honest words.
Strive to improve.
Life experiences.
Pondering my next poem.
Even though my eyes are heavy,
Type out one more line through the remedy.

7/2/25

A Seat At The Table

I give you rest
Conversation, influence Your invited
So much has time passed
Welcome in my home
At the table
You've walked many miles
Rest a while
Food to eat
Wine to drink
A long journey ahead
An old friend
Reminisce
Blessed or those who serve Give bread
No need for anything in return
A good Samaritan

4/9/25

About The Author In A Poem

My last name, Gadbois.
Originated from D'Arbois from France.
A Unique name.
Gadbois was known as a skilled craftsman.
Specializing in wood carving.
For years passed down through generations.
Families settled in Quebec, Canada. In the United States soon after.
Roots from working with your hands.
I've always been artistic.
From Genealogy to Ancestry.
From drawing to writing poetry.
A keen eye for detail.
On September the 18th, all turn 50.
I have a passion for writing poetry.
For years, I have enjoyed lifting weights.
(Investing in your health long term)
From grade school, I've always had a keen eye for drawing.
(1980's)
I started drawing tattoos in 2002.
(600 drawings)
After all these years, I'm still going to the gym.
At 27, I started riding motorcycles.
Motorcycles and writing poetry is freedom.
No one understands but me.
Just be yourself.

Unique in every way.
Follow your own path.
Be your own man.
Publish your own work.
Ride freely in the wind on 2 wheels.
Flying like a bird.
There is nothing like it.
Stay true.
Through encouragement.
For we are Writers.

7/2/25

Across the Water

A new hobby! What about fishing?
It's nice to sit in a chair while the fish are biting.
Who knows, maybe I will become a fisherman.
Throw out a line in the wind.
Be in the moment watching the water move across the way.
Have new memories of us fishing, I have to say.
What if this is our first date?
I love Mexican food, I don't want to be late.
Hand in hand we have the rest of our lives together.
It would be peaceful to cast out a line forever.
I wish I had more time when our hands are full.
What a wonderful day to spend time with you while the sky is blue.
Thanks for stopping by just to say hi.
Sometimes it's hard to live a lonely life.
Across the water is an open sky.
Together one day there are no good-byes.
You understand how hard my occupation is.
Through a simple hello, you have shown me kindness.
We could take a drive at night to see all the pretty lights.
It would be humbling to be with someone through the holidays.
Like a new chapter, these are new beginnings.
Maybe one day we could go fishing because the open water is so inviting.
Thank you for just being you. What if dreams come true?

All That I Am

All never leave you.
Thank you for giving me a chance.
Even though I've been through a lot.
All hold you up.
I remember our first date. It was kinda late.
Our first walk in the park.
The sun sets in indigo blue dark.
Our first dance.
The flames were gleaming.
A hug never to let go.
One day will grow old.
Maybe a few laughs.
All that I am.
I don't need anyone else.
I am yours.
Your heartbeat is mine.
You are the sky.
I am the night.
Never say good-bye.

12/17

An Amazing Son

I wouldn't trade you for the world.
I enjoy spending time with ya.
All my belongings will be yours one day.
You will carry out my last name.
I miss you when we're not together.
When I'm gone, I will still be with you forever.
You're growing up too fast.
Together we have a blast.
You're always eating all my food.
Never run out of nachos.
You're an amazing kid.
One day you will be a grown man.
I'm always here when you need me.
We could hang out and watch TV.
You have a great imagination.
You are my son.
One day, you can read all of my writings.
We can go out for some chicken wings.
You always make me laugh.
All the girls will be chasing after ya.
The apple doesn't fall far from the tree. You can be whoever
you want to be.

7/24

Another Sunny Day

Keep on writing
Another sunny day
Have it no other way
Rest under the shade
Always grateful
Always thankful
Be open-minded
Not pessimistic
I've gone through many changes
Great day to be alive
Just watching birds fly
Count your blessings
Wake up to the aroma of hot coffee
This is the day
That the Lord has made

3/6/25

Are You Still With Me

All give you a nudge
Can't even get a word out of ya
We've been together for a lifetime
I wouldn't change a thing
Are you still with me?
Days are flying by
You make my life shine
All hold you in the night
You bring the best out of me
What a wonderful journey
Growing old together
All wait for you on a beautiful horizon
There are no goodbyes
Leave smiles behind in the sky

4/13/25

Army Of 200 Million

During the end times.
Along the dried-up river called, Euphrates.
Make war against Israel.
3rd of mankind will vanish.
Jesus will return harped in white.
To establish his earthly kingdom with his might.
The end of the old.
Be ready, for there is no place to run.
All enemies of Israel will fall.
Dust shall return.
Fire burning all around.
Heaven will prevail.

Revelation 9-16

6/25/25

At Ease

Simple walk
Very few words
No worries
Every day is a blessing
Wise to knowledge
Proclaim anointed
Righteousness
Restore our soul
Be mindful of others
At ease through his understanding
Rest under his name
Live through faith
No stumbling blocks
Find your way back home
The Cross
Streams of rivers
Nourishment for the soul One day at a time
Content through the vines

8/11/25

Awe, So You Say part 2

A letter to you
I can't imagine walking in your shoes
Victorian time period
You're so fluent
Awe, so you say
Maybe some lavender tea
Nothing gets to you
You have it all together
Thank you for reaching out Your heart echoes
You bring out the best in me
Voices carry
Making up for lost time
You're like a sweet rose, so divine
Rhythm and soul
Awe, together we can grow
A new home
Never alone
Peaceful and cozy
Every morning with hot coffee

3/20/25

Awe, So You Say

Awe, so you say. I'm bewildered.
Ice on the rocks.
Amber to alcohol.
Your radiant smile.
Time departed.
A dance in the night.
Bring back old memories.
We drifted apart.
Gravity pulled so far.
A second chance.
Hand in hand.
You came back to me. Heaven was watching.
Maybe it's time.
Face to face under the velvet sky. Forgiveness is rewarding.
I just wanted to say that I'm sorry.
So much wasted time apart.
This time, I don't want to let go.

1/25/25

Because I Care

Nature, we are one.

Together, mild-tempered.

Through silent skies.

Just stare into your green eyes.

A wonderful person to be with.

Missing pieces.

Sometimes zealous.

All the mornings we have left.

With coffee, one day at a time.

With affections in the light.

Hold on tight.

Heaven waits.

Henceforth a long mile. Hold all of your smiles.

Another day to be close.

Because I care.

Sun down.

Always fun to be around.

Kick back.

Have some laughs.

Just be you.

Take a nap in the afternoon.

12/30

Before The Ink Runs Dry

Am I A Poet?
I have written #800 poems.
I thought I was an artist.
Creative illustrations.
Creative writings.
Changes passed the horizon.
I can't see everything in front of me.
A new chapter moving forward.
We are writers.
Deep thinkers.
Until the ink runs dry.
Always a pen in hand.
Pondering a new letter.
Poems are short stories.
Document your life.
Written in a journal, be inspired. Piano songs in the background.
Clouds floating all around. Maybe one last poem.
Before the sun goes down.
Eyes are heavy.
Candles are burning.
The love of poetry.

6/2/25

Beyond Content

I don't need anything
Can't complain
Thankful for one more day
I'm beyond blessed
I have rest
Free from all of my burdens
I'm growing into the old
Just trying to put the wrong things right
Someone can be an impacted in your life
Someone gave me a second chance
Beyond patience
Paint the sky beautiful colors
Our life is parallel forever
Move on from the past
New memories will last I'm beyond content
I don't need gold or silver Just being punctual
With you, I'm always true
When I'm gone
All wait for you
Through a song

4/15/25

Billionaires

Gain the whole world. Forfeit your own soul.
They idolize themselves. Alter ego.
Ultimate comfort lifestyle.
Manipulation.
Deceitfulness.
Accumulation, gathering of wealth.
Eternal priorities.
You can't take anything with you when you die.
Spiritual blindness.
Pride with arrogance. Power hungry.
The poor, walk on by.
Serve only yourself.
Control culture.
Dust shall return.

6/22/25

Bleak Conclusion (Soul Travel)

Cultivating escape

Travel on a smoky train

Destination approaching Window searching Are you with me?

Abundant open scenery

Emotions empty

Travel collective with embraced memories

Snapshot photography

Vacation long overdue

Dancing flowers animation view

Arms wrapped around freedom

Embarked poetry sink therapeutic

Wings fly upon azure air

Rhymes drown in rhythms

Minimized stained glass windows

Travel afar

Can't fathom many miles

A new journey captured

Bleak conclusion

Soul searching

Mind pondering

Life parallel

Travel here and there

8/14/25

Blood On The Rock

Sorrowful troubled moment.
Lift the burden.
May this cup be taken from me.
Soul overwhelmed by the. 30 silver coins of betrayal.
Hinder me before the storm.
Before the cross.
Blood on the rocks.
A lost world.
I knew your name even before you were born.
Soon anguish and suffering.
Alone above the sky on a tree at night.
First, pray for strength.
I tremble knowing what's upon me.
The betrayal. Lost disciple.
Everyone fled.
While I bleed.
Embarrass the cross with me. Garden of Gethsemane.

Luke 22:43-44

10/22

Blue Bird

Have you ever wondered what it would be like to fly?
To be free in the sky.
To let things go and not to worry.
To venture out, in color not to ask why.
Birds do not complain, But we do, all the time.
In chains we carry many burdens.
With pride, we lack discipline.
We have lost our way.
We just need some encouragement throughout the day.
Take in the moment to be thankful.
Be humble where you stand through principle.
Be still in the storm.
God will show you the way evermore.
Overcome with determination.
When life is hard don't cave in.
Walk the narrow road ahead.
Like a bird, they know they are fed.
Breathe in the fresh air after the rain.
After the storm has subsided, don't feel ashamed. Through hospitality, you have been a good friend.
After all these years, you have always been very genuine.
As the wind passes me by.
We will be together in time.

Matthew 6:25

Blue Bonnets

Purple Flowers
Velvet Clouds
Lupinus Collective March 7, 1901
Texas state flower
Pioneer on open fields
Blue-Bonnets reflects Beautification
Fields of blue as far as you can see
Some patches along the highway
During spring break
Family pictures
Family traditions
Capture the moment
Blue-Bonnets fly by on the open road
Diligence like a blue feather
Beautiful blue flowers painted like a picture
Just traveling through
Fields of Lavender
Never in someone's front yard Always miles apart
The wind moves the moment Time flies by in Velvet

3/25/25

Blue Print

Spiritual beginnings
Be patient, don't worry
Walk the narrow road
With very few words
Live a healthy life
Opportunity to rise
Blueprint to be true
Write down notes
Life with balance
Follow the cross
Don't follow the world
Don't cast out stones
You have a unique gift
This is your blueprint
Take it easy
Don't have to always be in a hurry
Don't compare to others
Don't worry about tomorrow
Be a star in the sky
Stand up and fly

3/14/25

Branch Of Knowledge

Seed takes root.
Plant good fruit.
Endeavor towards encouragement.
Alleviate pressure.
A branch of knowledge.
Water green gardens.
Upkeep, beloved.
Healthy rhythms.
Rendered toward spiritual nourishment.
Wisdom to calmness. No stress or worries.
Count your blessings.
Sun rises early in the morning.
Breathe in poetry.
A new day is refreshing.
Serene melody from within.
With humble beginnings.
A narrow road to the heavens.

6/30/25

Bridges Lead Us Somewhere

A new chapter in your life
A milestone symbolizes
Bridges unite
With no fight
Brings people together
Over green pastors
Live in the country
Work in the city
Arches to mountainous slopes
*Through canyons, A beautiful view Where does your bridge
lead you?*
Somewhere new
New roads
Where the water flows
Bridges leads us somewhere
From here to there
Maybe a new relationship
Symbolizes hope
New beginnings
To be set free
Whatever it means to you
Brings us together
Over troubled waters

3/10/25

Bridges

The world I know
I'm ready to let go
Implement toward change
Grow, I'm not the same A new path
Rest in emerald soft grass Slow to anger
No worries toward tomorrow
Over bridges
Gravity pulls
Down to earth
Be alert
Choices ajar
Beyond the stars
Be your own man
Journey through many colors With nothing to prove
Don't need anyone's validation
Just be you
Every day is a blessing
Bridges connecting

8/11/25

Brown Coffee Beans

Smell of hazel aromas.
River pecan flowers.
Polished wood varnished.
Brown garnet, with amber shades.
Chocolate mint delights.
Coffee spice nightly.
Evening fire roasting.
Axinite crystal luminous.
Brown-Eyed Susan. (flower)
Pine cone grain tarnished sharp edges.
Pencil tones veer, dust storms.
Brown coffee beans echo iron meadows.
With Tiger-Eye silver lining.
Autumn Fern (brownish fronds) burning.

7/3/25

Calming Rivers

Touch like a feather.
Flowing calming rivers.
Milky skies to ivory.
Heavenly dreams radiant.
Green gardens are so fluent.
Delicate like a rose peddle.
Serene blessings.
The old rugged cross I want to be.
Through heavy burdens he carries.
We are sculptured to serve.
.Stand strong in the dark storm.
Learn by example.
Be a mentor for others.
Calming rivers.
Be an ear to hear.

7/13/25

Candle Opera

Have you ever taken time out to look up at the stars?
They shine bright from afar.
Seeing light dancing at night.
Feeling spiritually grateful all the time.
Looking up, counting your blessings.
Through an orchestra, the wind is singing.
Guidance along the path.
Growing old, time goes by fast.
Reach out and touch the flames.
Like a vivid memory that will always remain.
Water resides down a stream.
Candle Opera has a symbolic meaning.
Don't take life for granted.
Through a song, listen to the message.
Take time out of your busy life.
From me I give you warmth in the moonlight.
I just wanted to show you my appreciation.
Thanks for giving me a chance through a colorful illustration.
You have been my inspiration till this day. My love for you will never fade.

3/21

Carry The Lamp

Through the noisy streets.
The darkest nights.
Through many burdens.
Recognize your salvation.
Do not complain.
Walk brave not knowing.
Potential to achieve.
Hath discipline, continue growing.
Carry the lamp.
Be open-minded.
Nourishment to the soul.
Be the light on a dark road.
Ignite the fire.
Have faith, move forward.

2/27/25

Casting Out Stones

Don't judge someone's mistakes.
Lift them up throughout the day.
Why cast out stones towards your brothers?
We've all been down this road before.
Help those in need.
Sometimes we bleed.
Some live through loneliness.
A life in the mist.
Leave the stones behind.
Lift someone up into the sky.
Be a friend to talk to.
Never a burden, push on through.
There is hope.
A brighter day to start over.
No stumbling blocks.
Protect you in the dark.

10/7

Chalk

White powder rock.
Just 45 minutes on the clock.
Teacher is the tool.
The chalk is the writer.
Many lesions, many words.
White dust across the blackboard.
Erase to smudge.
Chalk rewrites discipline.
Learn as much as you can.
Let poetry begin.
Refining thoughts.
Lost time writing in cursive. White limestone,
To a soft-smoked poem.

12/16

Climb Mountains

Shifting-Waters
Grateful-Deliverer
Beautiful-Skies
Healthy-Life
Old-Soul
Have-Control
Through-Patience
Stay-Influenced
New-Door
Brighter-Future
Climb-Mountains
Over-Abundents
Lost-Found
Music-Sound
Open-Minded
Shine-Bright
Vivid-Pictures
Bridge-Builder
Faith-Believer
Humble-Forever
Confidence-Alive
Suffer-Survive

9/4

Clock Humming

Clocks hands moving slowly
In no hurry
With no worries
Content and humming
Clocks chiming
Time wondering
With no company
Some people are the same
Parallel reminiscing
Color's fading
Time crawling
No complaints
Hearts content
No burdens
Take it easy
Just out of curiosity
Eyes are glazed
In a haze
Delirium sometimes
Clock humming
An ordinary day
Time passing by
Time chasing no one
Coffee early morning sun
A lonely life
Birds fling

Clocks tell time
Through the window, light shine
Just enough to get by

2/26/25

Clocks On The Wall

Pause to ponder
Clocks are timekeepers
Time fading away
Writing in a drought under the rain
Hues of time
Leaving shadows behind
Don't take life for granted
Clocks made with smoked wood
Time echoes
Harmony through gratitude
Drenched in amusement
Just writing you a letter with spice
With memories that will last a lifetime
Being sincere
Clocks on the wall
Time escaping
Hand in hand in a charcoal painting

5/5/25

Clouds In My Coffee

Just wondering.
Clouds in my coffee.
Wake up early in the morning.
Daydreamer.
Crisp morning air.
After the rain falls.
No plans.
Just my imagination.
Grateful for each day.
Hot coffee with steam.
No worries. Set free.
No drama.
No cell phone.
No problems.
Peaceful evenings.
A simple life.
While birds fly.
Just reading a book.
With deep thought.
Turn the page.
Mind racing.
Read cover to cover.
While the candles burn.
Take it easy.
Another poem in the morning.

2/16/25

Clouds Out Of Sight

He was taken up into the sky.
Clouds out of sight.
Return one day.
Brothers believe, live a holy life.
Rest on Sabbath day.
Stay humble and pray.
Witness on the land.
Have seen the Mount of Olives.
What an amazing event.
Never forget.
I am the ends of the earth.
Move through wonders.
Embrace the moment.
Look up to Heaven sent.
Walk the narrow road.
Speak the word.
Stand firm till the end.
Follow what you believe in.
He was hidden behind the clouds.
Return with a raging sound.
I am writing you my last
letter. I am with you forever.

Acts 1:9

9/30

Cocoon Uncertain

Used as a metaphor
Little green caterpillar
Transcends for the better
Hidden low for a while
Isolated for a short-term
Darkness to light
Time to mature and grow
Bright colors unknown
Crawl first, one day fly
Down in the valley, soon open sky
Cocoon open up to a surprise
Silent to mature
Many colors like a stained glass window
Free to observe
Patient to learn
Blossom to explore
We all came from the dirt
A little bit of guidance
But first calm isolation
Cocoon to fly
Another painted sky

8/21/25

Colorful Dreams

An open road is vibrant.
I'm humble walking beside ya.
What a wonderful life.
Across the water in the light.
Where do we go from here?
I made a wish and you appeared.
Maybe we have lots in common?
Always together, we have so much fun.
Through music and sound.
Sometimes we get lost in the crowd.
Colorful dreams will always be you and me.
Even if we don't always agree.
We could dive into many colors.
You saved me when I was under.
When life was lonely and black.
You took me by the hand.
I have truly enjoyed your company.
We could paint the sky
evenly. I just wanted to say
thank you.
For being so true.
What if it was meant to be?
Forever together in a dream.

6/13

Consumes Me

The air we breathe
Time sprint writing
A keen eye through poetry
Document in black ink
Mind always racing
Hand gliding across the page
Sometimes writers block, just pondering
Running out of time
Words written through Victorian vocabulary
Poetry consumes me
Write your own journey
Another pleasant letter complete
Morning aroma with flavored coffee
What about cursive writing?
New poems on the horizon
One more song to sing
Writing continues to consume me
Maybe I have P.T.W.D.
Post-Traumatic Writing Disorder
Just saying
Always a pen in hand
Always thinking
A poet's mind flying

3/27/25

Content Values

Don't need much
I can do without
Considerate of others
Open a car door for her
Many have lost their way
Morels don't mean a thing
Be courteous no matter how you're treated
Sometimes we are down in the valley
Take one day at a time
Mentor those to be prepared to fly
I'm just an old soul
Into the gray moving slow
No more weight to carry
No more worries
Retirement ahead
Heaven sent
Just a little bit of patience
With content values
Just living in a small simple house
Don't need to follow the world
Wise in my old age
Time is passing me by

8/11/25

Cool Breeze

Another cool breeze.
Leaves moving across the street.
Sometimes just day-dreaming.
I looked up, you were standing.
Cooler weather.
You held me closer.
Stranger no more.
Journey walking through nature.
You don't say much.
Maybe this is luck.
Another cool breeze.
No shoes, just feet.
Lean on me.
A beautiful horizon, is she.
The clouds hold our reflections.
Wake up, I must be dreaming.
Can't let go.
If true, hold you forever.

10/29

Creative Thoughts

Creative-Writings
Critical-Thinking
Committed-Dedicated
Characteristics-Virgo
Chatter-Soap Box
Courage-Self-Improvement
Comfort-Settle
Color-Horizon
Calling-Helpful
Chosen-One
Choices-Made
Clutch-Hold On
Cut-Heal
Corner-Turn
Candle-Light
Chess-Your Move
Chisel-Stone
Conversation-Friendship Challenging-Grow
Compromise-Agreement

9/12

Crooked House

Be content.
Don't take life for granted.
Crooked house.
Be you all around.
Sometimes pulling weeds.
Complaining, don't feed.
Through harvest.
It's a test.
Be content.
Each day is a gift.
Sometimes down in the valley.
Count your blessings.
Short on change.
That's O.K.
Grateful anyway.
Down to earth.
Don't ask for much. A crooked house.

11/6

Cup Overflowing

Don't be discouraged.
Be open-minded.
Wait your turn.
You're in the waiting season.
Be thankful for today.
The cup will overflow.
One day there will be an open door.
Be patient through a vivid picture.
Ascend and move forward.
You may face the storm.
Trust and transform.
Be grateful for a blessing.
From above, they are listening.
Your miracle is on the way.
Wait for the delivery.
Don't worry about what you can't see.
Be open to be set free.
An ancient door is open.
A cup will overflow when you're not watching.
The way maker.
Waves are calm in the water.

9/1

David & Goliath

Big vs Small
Pebbles vs Sword
David vs Goliath
Tall vs Short
Sling-Shot
Sword and Shield
Sheppards Boy
Giant to Sky
Just a few stones
On the battleground
Bravely won
Shepherd boy on the throne
Respect from the crowd
New King in town

12/20

Dear Heaven

Just writing you a letter.
I'm being sincere.
Life is lonely down here sometimes.
Everyone is hibernating.
No one understands me.
Show me the way.
Am I a poet?
I'm trying to walk the narrow road.
Sometimes there's no rain, my thoughts are in a drought.
Can't wait to go home, heavenly sky with no doubt.
Clouds will carry me with poetry.
I ponder what Heaven would be like.
A small house with a small room so I can write.
All have to wait a little longer.
One day I will pass on.
With a beautiful song.
(Flowers, by Helen Jane Long)
Show me the way.
We will meet through the radiant horizon.
With many colors someday.

6/8/25

December 10th, 1830

Born Dec. 10th, 1830.
Beautiful poetry.
E.E.D.
Lived in solitary.
Known for so many poems.
From Amherst, Massachusetts.
Her life is isolated.
Had one brother and one sister.
Greatest poet ever lived.
Emily Dickinson.
Passed away on May 15th, 1886. (age 56)
One faded picture.
Over 1,000 poems.
Vigorous writer in the shadows.

10/30

Deep Thinkers

Always writing.
Always thinking.
Over analyzing.
More poetry.
They all tell a story.
All have meaning.
Some have found their niche.
Maybe writing is a gift.
Keen eye for detail.
Write, free will.
Poetry and art.
Hand in hand together.
Art captures someone's talents.
I have five
tattoos. I love
drawing too.
In my 40s, I started writing poetry.
New poem every other day.
Emily Dickinson's birthday was yesterday.
(12-10-1830)
Deep thinkers keep on writing.
No writer's block today.
Document a new letter to read.
In us all is poetry.
Take time out from life.
Always something new to write.

12/13

Delicate Waves

Marble glass adorn.
Fog across the water repeal.
Delicate waves.
Reflections travel gracefully.
Past the horizon, echoes of amber through scenery.
Atmosphere painted beautifully.
Waters apart.
With delicate smiles.
Humbled shifting sands.
One day, we will meet again.

6/28/25

Deposit

Not Money.
Just knowing.
Deposit knowledge. Time
with your kids.
Understanding.
Balance out your life.
A healthy relationship.
Not selfish.
Strong work ethics.
Time well spent.
Not greed.
Clarity.
Encouraging words.
Stay focused.
A home.
A healthy lifestyle.
Quality.
Be uplifting.
Well-mannered.
Good morals.
No worries.
No burdens. Deposit.
Stay positive.
Not pessimistic.

2/18/25

Desert Poem

Always chasing the wind
Sweet sound soothing violin

Air dry, subdued quiet room
Poetic drift embrace gloom

Paper waits, ideas bend
Wrinkled clouds ascended

Just a small black desk
Embrace silent voices isolated

Mind runneth off the deep end
Desert poem heat index

Quench a poetic journey
Nightly shadows with creative scenery

No validation
Posted stamp flies freely

8/18/25

Detour

Lean not into your own understanding.

Gain knowledge, embrace.

With wisdom, be open-minded.

Can you pass the test?

Obstacles are only temporary.

Rough patches are part of learning.

Take a detour.

He gave us our name even before we were born.

Don't lay down stumbling blocks towards our brothers.

Be encouraged to move forward.

Give him the burden.

Have patience not knowing tomorrow. A new road with guidance.

The storm has passed,

Gain understanding from above.

Be a peacemaker.

Proverbs 3:5

6/23/25

Don't Forget About Me

Empty house
Silent sound
Simple soul
A letter for you
Horizontal at noon
Numb and alone
You're free in the sky
While I'm down here dying
Don't forget about me
Immune to longevity
Bone-white reminiscing
Mind diminishing,
Do you have room for me?
All put an ivory rose on your grave
Thinking of you every day
Don't worry about me
Portray true devotion
One day we will meet again
My last breath
My beloved

7/9/25

Don't Need Much

Live without wealth.
Have some bread on the table.
Remain humble.
Not above anyone.
Keep life simple.
Enough to pay the bills.
Walk the narrow road.
Live in solitude.
Don't need to be rich.
Nor famous.
Grateful to own my own house.
I live in the south.
Don't need much.
Just a few bucks.
Don't go into debt.
Just another burden.
Just me with some coffee. Count your blessings.

10/9

Don't Throw In The Towel

Equal opportunity
Biggest fight of your life

Last chance
Stand up to greatness

Hold on
All the hard work in the shadows

The final bell
You're a fighter

This is your time
Let nothing get in your way

When the dust settles
It's worth all of the effort

Stand alone at the top
This is what you we're born to become

3/17/25

Don't Worry About The Small Things

Life is too short to worry.
Burdens are exhausting.
Always stressed.
Water under the bridge.
We all have problems.
We are consumed.
Life can be overwhelming.
Even the small things.
Not knowing.
Leave your worries behind.
Do you trust in him?
Do you ever look above?
Sometimes, wonder.
We don't have all of the answers.
Waiting for a miracle.
Put your burdens in his hands.
He wants to carry our burdens.
We have to trust in him.
No matter how dark the road.
Don't have to suffer long.
Hard times to grow.
Tomorrow is a new day.
Be patient for his calling.
No more worries.
Find a way.
His way.

Matthew 6:25-34

_3/3/25_

Don't Worry

We all have many burdens.
Life can subside, I'm certain.
We carry too much by worrying.
For change be open-minded and willing.
I understand that we feel responsible for it all.
Too much anxiety at our jobs.
Be slow to anger.
Frustration won't last forever.
Sometimes we end up going down a hard road.
Some circumstances are out of our control.
Take time out to recognize change.
You can enjoy life without fame.
Keep life simple.
All things are possible.
Sometimes we need encouragement.
Listen to advice for improvement.
Kick back and have a cold drink on a rocking chair.
Be grateful for all the things you have, because one day it will all disappear.
Let the past go and move forward.
Put yourself last and serve others.
Life is rewarding when you give.
All those around you will appreciate it.
There's nothing like spending time with your kids.
Be down to earth and remain grounded.
We can face tomorrow.
One day in heaven, there will be no more sorrow.

3/18

Early Morning Interruption

Traveling steamed coffee
Aroma in silence

A lamp early dusk
Trees swaying are curious

Mountains embrace us
From afar

Just pondering ajar
Hinder early morning

Coffee gives me lightning
Wake up to another blessing

Leaves scattered
Poetry thoughts gather

Interrupted eye-catching
Overflow clouds dancing

6/25/25

Eloquent

Writing fluently.
Sighing wondrous.
Inhale thoughts.
Eloquent voices.
Vivid colors.
Cobwebs are artistic in a corner.
Pen bleeding black ink.
A ghost with haunted writings.
Beautiful song through melody.
Mind flowing.
Countless times in a haze.
Daydreaming, sun fades.
She writes another poem.
Fire burning in her soul.
Silver hair streak.
Green eyes can see.
Toil to the pen.
Another poem at hand.

1/26/25

Encouraging Words

Be uplifting.
Not pessimistic.
Use encouraging words.
Compassion for others.
Change someone's life.
Come back to say thank you one day.
Positive thinking rooted.
Set a new path, new direction.
Good soul shows through reflections.
Words of healing.
Chance to help someone.
Lift them up through confidence.
You can impact their future.
A blessing to be delivered.

10/30

Every day Is A Present

Be grateful for each day.
Hard work, make good grades.
Reveal treasurers.
Go beyond the naysayers.
Publish your talents.
Every day is a present.
Don't be pessimistic.
Stand brave in the mist.
Today, prevail.
Don't be in self-doubt.
Stand patient in the storm.
Yesterday may be gone.
Extinguish guilt.
Hard times won't last forever.
We all make mistakes.
Make a change.
Learn to grow.
A new letter in a vivid poem.
Smile, move forward.
Together, we have each other.

2/21/25

Fabric Torn

Lies and betrayed
Engulfed in flames
Never change
Torrent in vain
Ravished relationship strained
Underappreciated In disbelief
Your elusive implied
Mind all over the map
Fabric Torn
You never listened
Just broken
You can't breathe underwater
You never wanted my help
You never said sorry
You never needed me
Go your own way
All be in my grave
(Kids don't respect their parents these days)

4/8/25

Faith In The Shadows

What is discipline?
Words of wisdom
Knowing right from wrong
Deposit into a healthy future
Not to go down a hard road
To be respectful toward others
To build character
Become a messenger
Slow to anger
Being open-minded
Sometimes we run into a closed door
Sometimes you can't see around the corner
Learning patience
Faith in the shadows
Sympathy for others
A message through poems
Putting yourself last
Leave it all at the cross

5/12/25

False Idols Part 2

Arrogant people (celebrities)
Egos
Money
Spiritual decay
Engraved images
Self-indulgence Power
False statues
Silver and gold
A.I.
False idols that crumble
Shapeshifter
Deity to sand
All dust shall return
Consume everything you see
Flesh for the taking
Pride
Hopeless lies
You can't take anything with you in the end
Lose focus on the narrow road
Society will suck the life out of you
A race to be famous
Worship only yourself
To put your own flesh on a pedestal

7/6/25

False Idols

Mankind service idols in the flesh.
Their hearts are in darkness.
They strive to be just like them.
Take money for the kill.
They worship the world.
Take for themselves on schedule.
They chant their names.
They're all jealous of their fame.
Men covet what they see.
Only blinded by darkness and not free.
Mankind will become self-indulgent.
To only gain the whole world for themselves.
They waste money on entertainment.
Only to be a hero like the greatest.
The wants and needs are limitless.
In the end they will be empty-handed.
Worship the flesh to be someone else.
One day all your efforts will burn down.
Fueled by greed.
Soon they will be forgotten and buried six feet deep.
What a dreadful day of judgment.
Just to serve themselves above us.
No one can hear you from underground. We have moved on
without a sound.

4/24

Father To Son

You are blessed.
Well established.
I am beyond pleased.
I'm here whenever you need me.
We go through seasons.
Keep on believing.
Shine through rain.
No one to blame.
Be victorious.
Stand in your presence.
To the ends of the earth.
You are first.
Hold you up high.
Together we fly.
What a blessing you are.
Be humble and mindful.
One day you will understand.
I give you all I can.
Be wise on the narrow road.
Not far from home.

8/26

Psalms 1:7-8

Final Applause

Velvet drapery in the dusk background
A turntable goes around in sound
Baffled from the scenery
On stage imaginary
A final applause
Voices echo
The crowd lowered in the shadows
Blue lights array smoke A late-night show
The dark curtains open
Music in the background travel
Across the floor
Dancing sway amused
Put on a play
Live performance shadowy
A pleasant evening
A poem live compelling
The final applause
Standing ovation
A play greatly appreciated

5/23/25

Final Verse

Cloudless Sky
Closing Eye
Tied Crashing
Cities Sleeping
Poetry Re-writing
Gravity Pulling
Winds Silenced
Unspoken Words
Retired Burdens
Final Verse
Radiant Moon
Time Collapse
Memories Fading
Mountains Shifting
Air Bending
People dying
Time Ending
Heaven, New Beginnings

8/3/25

Four In The Fire

Summoned by society.
Don't follow greed.
Stand in bravery.
Smoke rubble in the sky.
Sometimes overwhelmed.
Trust in the dark.
Untouched from the furnace.
Long road traveler.
Beyond wanderer.
Boundless into the unknown.
Thyself, believe.
Shadows, break free. Ruin blazing fire.
Rise up, walk further. Soul searching.
Hath understanding.

11/7

Daniel 3:25

Free Verse Poems

Different style of writing
Last words don't have to rhyme
Any kind of topics
Written in your own words
Free verse documenting
Just another rainy day
Just be yourself
Nothing to prove
Characterized penmanship
Rhythm with no structure
Stanza patterns
Expression thoughts written down Literature to be published
Art and creative skills of handwriting
The love of poetry
Free style in vivid skies
Keep on writing into tomorrow
A new passion to follow Carefree poems
With a mechanical pencil

3/27/25

Giving

Has someone asked you for money?
The guy was humble you see.
We have a lot to be thankful for.
A hard life, some sleep on the floor.
Take nothing for granted.
A good feeling to give.
Better to give than to receive.
Be grateful to have food on the table.
Some lives are unstable.
Don't judge a hard man's life.
Evaluate your own from the inside.
Give back when you have the time.
Many are less fortunate than you.
Jesus served on foot too.
Show a humble example to your kids.
Something they will never forget.
Life is not all about material things.
Those who receive, will appreciate it.
The cost of living is overwhelming.
Be thankful that you are healthy.
One day you will be rewarded in Heaven.
Be a good Samaritan.

9/19

God Paints The Sky

Have you ever wondered what it would be like on the other side?
Take time out to give thanks, and not to be blind.
I believe that in the morning God paints a sunrise.
In the evening in many colors, he paints the sky.
Be grateful for all that he has given.
Do all things without complaining.
Don't follow the world and be materialistic.
We are just passing through at the moment.
Stand strong and symbolize the cross.
From above he's looking for the lost.
Be a mentor for those in need.
Be open-minded to change along a new path and receive.
He is waiting for us to come home.
In a dark world we are not alone.
Wisdom is nourishment to the soul.
Maintain scripture for what it's worth.
Every day we are here, it's a blessing.
He knows that burdens can be challenging.
Give all to him, for we are his.
For we are extraordinary with talents.
Show me the way on this journey.
Let the fire keep on burning.
We are the light like a lamp.
I was lost but now I am found.

11/26

Golgotha (The Place of the Skull)

You paid it all at Calvary.
The cross was planted in the ground suddenly.
Outside the Jerusalem walls.
It was the greatest suffering of all.
Alone on the cross.
Till this day, no one has forgotten.
Another cross on the left and on the right.
In darkness the lightning strikes.
The ground trembles on the hill of bones.
Through testimony, you will be sitting on the throne.
Three nails and a crown of thorns.
You knew me even before I was even born.
With a spear in your side, one day you will appear
and we can glide in the sky.
Through the red stripes we are all saved,
But it has to be a choice we all have to make.
Listen to a beautiful song standing on the horizon.
The tomb is empty, he has risen.
Sin has been buried for those who still believe.
He said, It is done for you and me.

3/21

Good Standards

Generous

Courteous

Manners

Meaningful

Respectful

With Balance

Encouragement

No Conflict

Honest

Dependable

Good Standards

Noble

Good Spirited

Patient

Good Morals

Good listener

Positive Compass

Understanding

Open-minded

Don't take life for granted

Good Samaritan

4/20/25

Green Gardens

Always with gratitude
Remain grounded
A place to gather
Green Gardens
Colorful glaciers
Gold hue's glow
Humble with grace
Above with glory
A geometric gift
Welcome as a guest
Relax with ginseng tea
Be grateful to the
Past the horizon agaze
No grief to the grave
Beautiful green gardens
Be one with God

3/15/25

Halos In The Mist

Golden rings of dim lights.
Soon to fade after dawn from night.
Cobblestones staggered down a crooked path astray.
Halos in the mist acknowledge a mystery.
Haunted places with roaming ghosts.
Halos to lemon quartz allures.
Fluent lights circles.
Take a stroll in the abandoned dark.
Just pondering past vivid shadows.
With loneliness all around.
Do you ever look up and wonder?
Maybe halos guide us in the dark.

6/19/25

1:15 am

Hard Working Hands

Never at rest.
Be your best.
Busy bee.
Always working.
Sometimes for others.
Nothing in return.
Hard-working hands.
Carpenter to craftsman.
Hammer and nail.
Another home built.
Food on the table.
A roof to cover.
Work hard another day.
Rest under the shade.
Time is short.
Just growing old.
Hands never rest.
Working until his death.
Wrinkles in his face.
A smile in the rain.

12/30

Have Mercy On Me

Compassion and forgiveness.
I have fallen short in the end.
Have mercy on the day of judgment.
What a blessing through human emotions.
Exit punishment.
He paid for our sins on the cross.
Repent and change your ways.
Returneth on the right path through glory.
Eyes are windows to your soul.
Pottery sculpture is molded into a beautiful vessel.
Parish underground for only a season.
Rise with him beyond the clouds.
I was blind to my own understanding.
I'm only human, for he walks with me.

Luke 18;38 Luke 18:43

6/30/25

Have Peace In Your Life

No struggles.

With no wants and needs. Be sentimental.

Simple through melodies.

Each day is a blessing.

Grateful sound sympathy.

Have faith in the dark.

Have peace in your life.

Be kind to your brothers. I'm thankful for my sight.

Travel soothing waters.

Calm with eyes closed in the storm.

It is just.

He has risen for us.

Nails on the cross.

Once I was lost.

Our new life has just begun.

He is the only way.

Through understanding, we are saved.

7/13/25

Have Rest

Trees swaying.
Thoughts pondering.
With fragile leaves.
Turning red and orange falling.
Seasons change.
Somehow always writing.
Sunset refreshing.
New ideas, daring.
For now silence, just resting.
Pen sleeping.
Poems subsiding.
Empty pages waiting.
Literature is fading.
Eyes closing.
Coffee, early morning.
Another whimsical day for writing.

6/8/25

He Saved You And Me

The world is cruel.
Always throwing stones.
Rage on the attack.
What happened to everyone?
Society is going mad.
Forgive our brothers.
He sees no color.
He calls us home.
Everyone's blood is red.
Life is short, we will all vanish.
Watch for the signs. Heaven
is so divine.
No other place that I would rather be.
He saved you and me.
Lift each other up.
Surrender through a hymnal song.
He paid for our sins.
One day we will meet again.
An open sky.
We are all invited by and by.

7/13/25

Heavy Burdens

Always under pressure.
With heavy burdens.
Sometimes you're running out of daylight.
Consumed by responsibilities.
Running low on energy.
Unexpected loss through grieving.
So much on your plate.
Never have a chance to breathe.
Time is always flying.
Kids are always needy.
Never time for yourself.
No choice but to carry on.
Dwelling toward tomorrow.
Too much laundry, another load.
Find rest in the shade.
For this day the Lord has made.
I will give you rest.
I will carry the weight of your burdens.

6/21/25

Matthew 11:28-30

Highway To Heaven

Sometimes we fall away.
With stubbornness, we follow our own way.
Focus only on ourselves.
We have forgotten our purpose.
To serve others.
Put my own problems on the back burner.
No more complaining.
Too much anxiety.
Halt toward your worries.
Voices silent carry.
Listen with your heart.
Carry the cross.
Highway to Heaven.
Make changes toward helping others.
Your story is not over.
A new chapter.
Be a good Samaritan toward your brothers.
Follow the narrow road.
Grateful with very little.

7/14/25

Hold Me Up

With conscious effort
Getting older
Forgetting, mind-wasting
Mind fading and aging
We need a reminder
Vacant thoughts
Write down note
Set your alarm clock
Can't remember
Be with me when I grow older
Sometimes I have writer's block
Can't recall
Trying to stay sharp-minded
Whatever time we have left
You're the remedy in my life
Hold me up
I'm four years older
Grateful for 20 years
You were always there when I needed you
Take time to enjoy the moment

5/12/25

Hold On

Hold on to the truth.
Through the sky he believes in you.
We hold old-fashioned values.
Find the lost, they will follow.
Abounding in joy, live freely.
Sin divides us, but he still loves you and me.
With knowledge give back your time.
Like a plant, you are the vine.
We all have potential to carry the cross.
As a student, we learn from the start.
Observe and be humble.
Give thanks and pray so we do not stumble.
In darkness, show me the way.
Walk with Jesus with no delay.
When you were only 12 you were in your father's house.
You are the remedy when I'm lost, now I am found.
Your kindness is limitless.
On one knee it's time to commit.
On this journey you walk beside me.
At the cross we can now see.
Forgive me for my days are numbered.
Through your sacrifice., you are with me forever.

11/1

Hebrews 10

Horizon Painted Nightly

Sun echo fades
Sky ends golden flames
Wistful evening
Winds cool untamed
Birds glide, never sleep
Horizon pained nightly
Clouds dancing wide awake
People sound asleep dreaming
Stars glitter, to river streaming
Silver reflections gleaming
Waves hum soothing
Heaven sky above watching
Tomorrow a beautiful day
Leaving behind another yesterday
Lullaby morning coffee
The love of poetry
We can truly see

8/3/25

House Built Upon The Rocks

Stand strong toward the storm.
With stones, be merciful.
Speak words of encouragement.
Through counseling and discipline.
Harvest uplifting fields.
Be mindful of others.
Be bold with integrity.
Streams of water flow patiently.
House built upon the rock.
Guard your soul in the dark.
Deliver from distress.
Be humble like the mountains.
The cross is the only way.
Walk with me through the valley.

Matthew 7:24

6/22/25

House Of Bread

Upon a humbled road ahead
House Of Bread
Abundance

Symbolic
A place of rest
Meaningful traditions

Spiritual beginnings
Mountains to valleys
Ancient pathways

Pilgrimage engraved
Passionate
Devotion

Put yourself last
Therapeutic
Give to others
Nothing in return

8/20/25

I Shall Not Want

A polluted world.
Fame and fortune.
To be idolized.
The car of my dreams.
To live outside my means.
I shall not want.
Be humble at heart.
Not to be arrogant.
I'm content where I stand.
Have guidance through the Emerald Garden.
Don't worry about tomorrow.
Just a few encouraging words.
Sense of peace through gratitude.

Psalm 23:1

6/14/25

I Surrender All

Be grateful.
For the food on the table.
Show me the way.
Have patience through the day.
I shall not want.
I surrender all.
Pray for the lost.
Keep holding on.
Remember these simple words.
Hold up the light in the dark.

10/1

Impatient

I have always been impatient.
Always independent.
Always in a hurry.
Never take time out to breathe.
I want things done my way.
Never take a break.
I am a Virgo.
September you know.
I am a perfectionist.
Always trying to do my best.
No room for errors.
With strong work ethics.
This is just me.
With ambition toward achieving.
Don't quit when you're on a mission.
Carry many burdens.
Be unique in your own way.
Work hard every day.
Never wanted to be anybody else.
Stand up tall, just be yourself.
Always under fire.
Through this journey, I am a writer.

7/30

Improvement

Don't be discouraged.
Don't complain about yesterday.
Be open-minded.
Be committed.
Stay dedicated.
Be creative.
It's worth the wait.
Even with no sign.
Don't be negative.
Be fortunat.
Think of others.
A believer.
Stay focused.
Work towards improvement.
Be patient.
Don't give up on your dreams.
May be surprised around the corner.
You might meet the right person somewhere.
Wait for a breakthrough.
Move on from negative people.
Change into a new season.
One day it could happen.
Work hard toward your goals.
Press on and be bold.

10/6

Indigo Mood

Skies azure chilling
Birds freely gliding

Zealous hues
Indigo mood

Short drive around town
Growing up in a small house

Fall burnt colors
Leaves wonder everywhere

Miscellaneous places
Afternoon walks

Independent thoughts
Songs travel on

Melody through smiles
Past paintbrush fields

6/25/25

Ink Hues On A Winding Road

Chapters turning
Leaves falling
Story telling
Intrigued animation serine
Deeper in every page sink beneath
Verge of complex themes
Rewrite unbound verses
Limitless parallel rendered
Lost in absurdities
Books for miles dusty planted in libraries
Sophisticated torrent
All the effort is worth it
Writers block
Brainstorming your thoughts
Achieve novel narratives
Ink hues on a winding road
Written passionate
The love of poetry
Turn every page, uncertain mystery
Dig deep, unfold in suspense journey
Walk with the author on the other side
With greenish sunsets with mint coffee

8/18/25

Into The Red

Into the red
Too much debt
Cost of inflation
Barely surviving
Under pressure
Too many burdens
Living paycheck to
paycheck
A dying civilization
No food in the fridge
A hard road to live
Some are homeless
We are just taxed to death What is the message?
Can never save up enough money
For a rainy day
Underpaid and under-appreciated
Need a break through
Maybe a miracle
Trying to be reasonable
Just to put food on the table
Work hard every day
To make ends meet
Writing down what is in front of me
I'm not the only one
Just wanted to be honest
Tomorrow is a brighter day

This won't be forever, I have to say
We all need a raise
Some hope to survive
Another hungry night

3/31/25

Iron Sharpens Iron

Telling the truth
Something they don't want to hear
Being a Sharp tool
Just being honest
Building up character
True friendship
Pay careful attention
Iron Sharpens Iron
A sharp metaphor
A blacksmith making orange sparks
Amber sparks to grow
Become the new you
Be the best you can be
This is a new day
Be a better man
Through the storm
A new person is born
Shape metal to iron
Become a better-equipped man Stand tall
Sharper than your adversaries

4/21/25

Is 30 Silver Coins All I'm Worth?

Is money all you want?
Don't walk away from the cross.
What is 30 coins worth?
What am I worth to you?
I gave you life.
You were betrayed with a lie.
You surrendered yourself to the world.
I was handed over for just 30 shekels.
As a brother, I haven't forgotten you.
You left me behind with an army that was brutal.
I walked on water.
You replaced me with silver.
I am the way.
Through greed, like dust you have faded.
I could have saved you.
You choose to go down the wrong road.
I have risen above the clouds.
You are now dust in the ground.
I was exchanged for very little.
I will bring down fire upon the world.
My suffering was unbearable.
I have always been with you.
One day we will meet again.
I will pass judgment toward men.
You cannot serve both God and money.
You have turned against me, so the world keeps on burning.

Matthew 26:14

7/12

It Is Well

Be humble.
No more sorrow.
Strive to learn.
Beautiful day tomorrow.
Rest on sabbath day.
Count your blessings.
Ask for forgiveness, no shame.
Absentee toward darkness.
Be the light at dawn.
Walk the narrow road.
A little bit of hope.
Don't ask for much.
Sometimes loneliness.
Strive to improve.
Be useful.
Put in the work.
It is well.
Just be you.
No one else.
Don't compare.
Run your own race.
Do your best every day.

2/16/25

Jerusalem On The Rocks

One day, when all of the nations are against me
World powers on the Earth are full of rage
They gather around Jerusalem in war
I will make Jerusalem an immovable
rock, into tomorrow.
All those who try to destroy her, will fail
Have a watchful eye over Judah from above
Be a follower of Jesus
Watch for me in the clouds
They will all turn to dust like the fallen
One day we will meet again
'Not one stone will be on top of another
A new Heaven and a new Earth
Sin will be gone forever
All those who stand with me will live 1,000 years

Zechariah 12:3

4/1/25

Judging Others

Think of others.
Don't pass judgment.
Don't compare.
You're no better.
All become dust in the end.
Loneliness needs a friend.
Harder life than yours.
You didn't walk in their shoes.
Lift them up.
Help them in crisis.
Be a heavy lifter.
Set a new path for the lost.
Be humble.
All have imperfections.
Good samaritan.
Nothing in return.

11/10

Just A Messenger

Sometimes we swim in a drought.
Disappointed with no doubt.
Always expecting.
Always in a hurry.
Wanting everything our way, this instinct.
Learn a new lesson.
Stand still, be patient.
He turned water into wine.
The sun rises to shine.
Have courage.
Through the hard times.
Be delivered unexpectedly.

6/23/25

Just As I Am

This was a great song to sing.
Back in the day, I do believe.
Just yesterday was so long ago.
Just like fishing, it's where the river flows.
I remember living in my first house.
I miss those days living in a small town.
Going to church every Sunday was a great memory.
Being young and so carefree.
Time has gone by so fast.
I wish the good old days would last.
"Just As I am", I look into the sky.
One day we will be lifted up so we can fly.
No going back to the old.
You can only wonder what we will face tomorrow.
Where do we stand in a song?
I've missed you while you were gone.
I just wanted to say I miss your smile.
Together we walked a long mile.
I will never forget the nice things you've said.
You look so lovely dressed in red.
No matter how lost I was back in the day.
You came back to show me the way.
I'm sorry I never said the words you needed to hear.
Together we watched the sunset by the pier.

5/23

Just The Way You Are

We first met so long ago.
Our first date was at Sonic you know.
You were so giving.
You were always patient with me.
I would read your letters.
Next to you, you made me better.
You had green eyes and beautiful hair in the sun.
We held hands and had lots of fun.
I'm sorry if I was ever selfish.
We both have been through many changes.
I will always be here when you need someone to talk to.
Beyond the horizon, you will always be beautiful.
Just the way you are is all you need to be.
You have always brought the best out of me.
It has taken too long to wake up and see.
We could always share some coffee.
I know we both have moved on.
I don't want you to ever feel like you're alone.
You have been the best mom in the world.
We've had great memories under the clear sky in blue.
Just take one day at a time.
You are the lamp, so never turn out the light.
Thank you for everything you did.
So many years have passed, all never forget.

4/12

Kindly Numb

Don't need much.
The soothing weather is calm.
Simple movement.
Piano mist with colorful rhymes.
New beginnings.
Time out to reminisce.
Undivided attention.
No particular reason. Fly through silent air.
Sometimes absent-minded with a glare.
Kindly Numb.
With so many blessings, too many to count.
Humble roots.
No worries for tomorrow.
Peaceful remedies.
Therapeutic hobbies.
Just sleep.
Lay low, like a feather.
A delicate afternoon.
The wind carries my soul.
One day I will be gone.
A new place far beyond.

7/7/25

King Of All Lies

The darkness in
disguise.
King of all lies.
Power of controlling.
With superhuman abilities.
Stubborn in every way.
A new lie every day.
Don't sell your soul for the world.
Another temptation
uphill.
Staring with daunting red eyes.
Shattered dreams left behind.
Another test in the desert.
No bread nor water.
A secret between you and I.
Evil creature on the rise.
Stand strong in the light.
Fight back with all your might.
Move on from your stubbornness.
You are better than this.
Leave your worries behind.
Don't listen to all of their lies.
Don't become one of them.
Become your own man.
Hope you understand.
Don't fall into the quicksand.

9/13

Last Prayer

If I don't make it to the sky,
Take my son who is mine.
He looks like me.
With many memories.
I don't have to give him the world.
Creative and wonder.
I can't live forever.
I'm growing into the gray faster.
All my writings are his.
Give him the sky when I'm dead.
I'm next in line.
Aches and pains are mine.
Ashes fade in the wind.
My life ends, my sons begin.

10/30

Lavandula

Purple fields.
Lavandula through the meadow.
As far as the eye can see.
Beyond breathtaking.
Above violet skies.
Morado organic shine.
A fragrant herb.
Also an Ametrine stone.
Lavender symbolism, old ways.
Cool breeze, open range.
Relieving stress purplish oils.
Recipe soothing gardens.
Lavender resembling.
Humble, soul searching.

11/6

Leaves, Too Many To Count

The wind moves them from place to place.
In my backyard, there are too many trees.
Too many leaves.
Waste of my time picking them up.
Better things to do, you know.
Always writing.
Leaves, too many counting.
Ready for cooler weather.
Open breeze, drive somewhere.
Leaves travel.
Take time out.
Count your
blessings.
Drive passed pine trees.
Open spaces.
Leaves, brown, orange and red.
Just thinking.
Just chilling.
Time of the year.
Leaves are everywhere.

10/18

Let The Guilt Go

Rebelled down a hard road

We all rebelled against our parents (1980s with a wooden spoon)

Every generation

Through adult-hood

I failed college

A divorce

Yep, child support

Bankruptcy

Just being honest

Disappointed in me

I'm under construction

Another detour

Let the guilt go

Always room to grow

Don't beat yourself up forever We all make mistakes

Sometimes we're in the valley

Always learning

Life is traveling

Seasons are changing

Wisdom to gain

What a crazy journey it has been in my shoes

Be an instrument

Sculptured into the new you

Lead by example

Let the guilt go

I've been down so many trials and errors
Trying to make it on my own
Don't feel guilty to ask for help
Family is always there
Admit I have a problem
This is between you and God Go back home to the Cross

8/27/25

Let There Be Light

Darkness hovering over emptiness
Let there be light, and it appeared
Morning to evening
Water separated from the land
Sky above hallowed ground
Light was all around
Colorful bodies of water for miles
Trees planted in the ground
Beautiful flowers breathe all around
Everything made is good
What if there were no people?
And no creatures
There would be no nakedness
No temptation
No sin
No one living
No one dying
No chaos
No crime
No money
No murder
A quiet place
The Garden Of Eden
A peaceful place
Where no one deserves to be.

<u>Genesis 1-3</u>

3/27/25

139

Lilies Of The Fields 1963

A field full of flowers.
Yellow is my favorite color.
Run freely in the wind.
Stay young with an imagination.
Be carefree through the open land.
Live a simple life if you can.
There's nothing like living out in the country.
This is the way it should be.
Swing high into the sky.
Don't let anyone else tell you otherwise.
Put on a beautiful song.
Play outside all day long.
Have an adventure just for fun.
Stay young under the sun.
It's just a small house above the hill.
An open field with lilies to feel.
What a wonderful life living on the farm.
With so many memories that are remarkable.
Walk with me in the open fields.
Maybe true love will be revealed.
Stay with me, into tomorrow.
When I look up, it has always been you.

6/13

Lost In A Book

A place to escape.
Hidden away.
Use your imagination.
What happens next?
A story to read.
A book to sink in.
Alone at home.
Smell of an old book.
Document your own writings.
Become an author, be surprised.
Always a deep thinker.
Turn the page.
New lines to read.
Write your own story.
Walk your own journey.
Lost in a book.
Plant your own garden.
Learn new words.
Knowing, builds character.
Eyes become heavy.
Fighting to stay awake.
Just one more page.
A bookmark to save your place.
So many words on a page.
Retain a great story.
Get lost in a book.

You can learn so much. Maybe a bookworm.
Write your own poem.

2/16/25

143

Marvelous Revelation

Beyond my sins.
He paid it all.
He calls us home.
No matter how far we're lost.
Show me the way.
In the valley it is just a season.
Marvelous Revelation.
A road to eternity.
Blood stained on the cross.
I surrender all.
Even though I'm stubborn.
He still loves each and every one of us.
He suffered on the rugged cross.
He already knew us even before we were even born.
What a Marvelous Revelation. A Marvelous Miracle.
He walks with us in the storm.
Melodies through our soul.

7/14/25

Melody Smile

Subtle expressions
Delay, helpless pause
Shyly into a haze
A Melody Smile
Softly quiet
A simple home
Empty pages Empty rooms
Narrow to solitude
Always reading Victorian books
Blushing bashfully
Just wondering What is your name?
I pass by you all the time
So brittle like snow
So dreamy through a stained glass window All hold all of your smile
All walk with you through whimsical clouds
A Melody Smile
A shyly girl
Breathtaking in a small town

5/8/25

Midnight Star

Radiant night
Darkness takes flight
Candles with a low dim light Star's
glow bright
Oceans crash on the rocks
Moonlight on the docks
Your reflections tread across the water
Stand by you forever Take me under
Black sky watches over
A second chance
Together at last
You are Midnight Star
It's burns from afar
Your green eyes sparkle in the night
Dust we become out of sight
Never take you for granted
True love that will last
Time is passing
Remember our memories
Look at the stars at night
Together until the end of time

3/11/25

Move Mountains

Beginning to the end
Eternity in the wind
Oceans crash
Mountains stand
Beautiful horizon
No boundaries
Beyond the sky
Leave the world behind
Wonders are beyond
I was appointed from day one
Soon my years will be gone
Dust shall settle upon the mountains

3/15/25

My Words Echo

I won't be here forever
One day, ascend through Azure clouds
I'm running out of time
Born to write poetry
Just pondering
Leave all of my writings behind
Save them for my son to read
Running out of ideas
Sometimes, writer's block Can I write you a poem?
They all have meaning you know
Pen, always writing
Ink, always bleeding
Thoughts, always scrambling
Document your life
Words written in a journal
My words echo
Melody through a piano
Echoes unbound
Just writing you a letter
One day, all be dust everywhere

4/24/25

No Umbrella In The Rain

All save all of your smiles.
Together, walk a long mile.
Your smiles in the rain.
We think the same.
Never in a hurry.
My eyes are blurry.
You walked in my path.
Dreams, our journey will last.
No umbrella or shade.
You're radiant every day.
The one I can't live without.
Hold your heart in a music box. Songs we can dance to.
Leisure in the rain, I'm dazzled.
You walked in my shoes.
We need each other to get through.
You held me up in the dark.
Sentimental, hugs are true.

11/3

Ocean Front

What a wonderful place to be.
A place to retreat.
Streams of current.
The sky is transparent.
Awake every morning.
Waves keep turning.
Fresh air to breathe.
The soul can rest at ease.
The morning sun is radiant.
The sun on your face is gorgeous.
Stand by your side.
Send forth to glide.
Can't thank you enough.
You gave us a chance.
Walk hand in hand.
Our footprints are in the sand.
Nothing like an ocean front.
I am grateful and beyond.
You're the one that binds us.
Through sustain and trust.

8/20

One Last Poem

Just turn the page.
It is blank.
Write another letter.
Your life is not over.
Keep on writing.
New ideas are always on my mind.
Sometimes I wrestle with my thoughts.
Sometimes I have writer's block.
Writing has always been a part of me.
Writing on paper, black ink.
Never waste a day.
Document your life in the shade.
This is your journey.
The love of poetry.

9/15

Only Human

How many poems?
How many problems?
How many bills?
Always worrying about tomorrow.
Encouragement is needed.
Open-minded.
Today is a new day.
Don't hold onto yesterday.
Locked up in prison.
Learn a lesson.
Learn to grow.
A better you.
Trials and errors.
Stand strong in the storm.
Don't be discouraged. We are only human.

12/14

Open-minded

More rain.

No one to blame.

Going through the seasons.

Standing in the storm.

Be open-minded.

Hard times are never permanent.

Door ajar.

Worry no more.

Balance, forward.

A breakthrough.

Set an example.

Encourage others.

Share your story.

Give some wise advice.

Courage-stabilize.

Pass the test.

Troubles won't last.

Don't be discouraged.

Just a short time.

It's greener on the other side.

Walk through the storm with me.

Be brave.

No worries.

Become a better man.

Learning a new lesson. Only humans.

Pain won't last forever. Trials and errors.

Just being supportive.
Just being observant.
You're not the only one with problems.
Send a blessing to others.

2/19/25

Over Yonder

You are very independent.
Camp out on the living room couch.
We may not always be together.
You're content over yonder.
Take time out to read a book.
Laid back under a roof.
Have some downtime.
Shades with a dim light.
Lazy on a rainy day.
Just wondering what you're thinking.
Just be you.
Always down to earth.
Surrounded by colorful pages.
You're unique in every way.

10/7

Passion For Writing

Soothing Words.
Pen glides across the silk paper.
A passion for writing.
Ironically the next line.
With instrumental music in the background.
Calming as rain falls.
A journey through literature.
Tunnel vision with words.
Writing through rhythm and harmony.
Was I born to illustrate poetry?
Black ink bleeds off the pages.
Strive to sharpen your skills.
Azure clouds ponder revealed.
Writing is therapeutic.
For we are poets.

6-22-25

Peace Maker

Don't need an argument.
Move forward.
Negative people will drain your energy.
Avoid the enemy.
Don't waste your time.
Move into the light.
Can't solve everyone's problems.
Just more stubborn obstacles.
Sometimes a door will close.
Open to a new road.
Pick your battles.
Some are not worth it.
Be a peace-maker.
I'm just a messenger.
Don't hold a grudge.
Don't complain like a crutch.
Rest without worries.
Be humble and free.
No gossip.
No Drama.

10/21

Pearl Waters

No shoes
Two souls flying parallel
Just barefoot in the sand
Pearl waters fluent
Souls running free
Sky indigo glowing
Silver ripples amazed
Zenith mesmerized
Celestial emerald lands divided
Open winds collide
You're the one who stands beside me
Grow old together heavenly
Take in the moment
No one can ever replace you
Hand in hand on the seashore
The one that I adore
Never hesitated
One day, we will ascend

6/25/25

Pillar Of Salt

Do you know the story of Sodom and Gomorrah?
Let me tell you.
Two cities destroyed from wickedness.
Only one family fled to the mountains.
Anger provoked by the sins of men.
Ancient cities in the sand.
A crime against nature.
Disobedience toward each other.
Evil throughout the streets.
People giving burnt offerings.
Soon there will be stones raining down.
Spare no one with fire and brimstone.
Grave sin to mankind.
Through homosexual, all will suffer and die.
The city and roads became a furnace.
No one was left.
Dominion of judgment.
This is Sodom and Gomorrah.
She turned around to look.
She became a pillar of salt.
The world is falling apart.
A sinful nation to the grave.

(Genesis 19:23-26)

7/25

Poem 4

Don't be afraid of loneliness, I am here Even though we are
miles apart, don't shed a tear.

We both belong as one

One day, we will be under the

sun. Don't fall apart where you

stand Soon we will be hand in hand.

Be strong when there's a storm Remain patient, for I am at your
door.

Wherever the journey takes you Your words you say to me are
true.

No matter how heavy your heart may be

All your burdens belong to me. We have

been together for a short time Someone

so beautiful is so kind. You have

sacrificed so much I long for your touch.

I love the blue reflections in your hair

No one can take from us what we have shared.

I will embrace the moments that you desire

Together as one, you are the fire.

A hard road you have survived,

In your path you deserve to have it all in the sky.

At the crossroads we will meet.

Where you stand, roses will be at your feet.

You surround me with love, I asked, and you were given from
above.

I will dedicate my life to you

You are so mesmerizing in blue.

When we met for the first time, I wished
upon a star, you would be mine.
I will never forget the words you say
You always take my breath away

Poetry Through The Storm

Trembling waters.
Oceans between us.
As far as the eye can see.
Waves crashing.
A long voyage with anxiety.
Trust and believe.
Stand still in the storm.
Look past the horizon.
Birds fly past above the lightning.
Poetry through the storm.
High tides towards encouragement.
Writing through a thundercloud.
Humble in the wind.
Stay calm in the raging storm.
Cry no more.
Dawn is near.
Shed no tears.
All raise you up from bondage.
Stand on mountains.
Side by side standing on water.
Write poetry through many colors.

Philippians 2:14

1/28/25

Praying Over Food In Public

Carry on the tradition.
Praying over your food in public.
Don't be ashamed of his name.
Don't worry about what strangers say.
Carry the cross.
You don't answer to the flesh at the end.
Show by example.
Spiritual nourishment is parallel.
Pass down your value.
Be humble at the table.
Thank him for each day.
Be grateful for many blessings.

6/23/25

Prevail

Do you have a disability?
We all have an opportunity.
Don't be so hard on yourself.
We can all prevail.
I know that sometimes we can be frustrated.
Believe in yourself, be patient.
Life is not easy.
You don't have to live in misery.
Don't worry about everyone else.
Just be you, I wanted to address.
The future is yours.
You can open up any door.
Don't worry about making mistakes.
We can all relate.
Stay upbeat and positive.
Stay motivated.
You have only one life.
Don't waste time.
All your hard work won't go in vain.
God calls you by your name.
Just live in the moment.
With your talent, be an instrument.

6/16

Pyramids Of Gold

Many moons ago.
Gods of stone.
Thrones made of gold.
Pharaoh boasted.
Temple writings.
Ziggurats. Monarchs.
Windows to the sky.
Ancient history forgotten.
Pillars of salt.
Gods will fall.
Concubine wives.
Yellow bricks stacked high.
Tombs of the dead.
All turn into sand.
False gods. False idols.

1/17/25

Quenching Rest

Reaching out for nourishment.
Dehydrated soul.
Quenching rest.
Deprived state of mind.
Burdens, constant bleeding.
Worn-out bodies.
Waves of worries.
Symptoms of loneliness.
You're compelled for soul-searching.
Come to the cross.
Thirst for nothing else.
Walk in the spirit.
Humble and hydrated.
Growing wisdom.
Righteousness.
Free from guilt.
New beginnings.
Pour your burdens on him.
We are only human.
Count your blessings.
Heaven is waiting.
There is no shame asking for help.
You're not the only one in a drought.
Sometimes we are down in the valley.
Have faith for a blessing.
Hard times are only for a season.
Brighter days are on the horizon.

7/18/25

Rachamim
(Compassion Of Mercy)

Why do nations rage?
Always at war in vain.
The wicked will never stop.
They love violence and it's wrong.
Under the sun, always at war.
No care for another soul.
What life is this?
No victory in the blood of violence.
It is in our nature to destroy ourselves.
Leaders care for no one else.
The fall of mankind.
Burn down all the land from the inside.
Very few people are left.
Hope Jesus remembers me in the end.
I want no part of this dark world.
Always another war.
Have compassion for those who still believe.
Through mercy, forgive me.
Time is like Sodom and Gomorrah.
One day it will be all over.
Judgment will be worse than before.
Not water but fire.
Raise up into the colorful sky.
All the cities will be burning bright.

7/13

Rain Man

I'm sorry that I have so many problems.
You helped me move into tomorrow.
You never felt sorry for me.
Always there in need.
I don't want to be a burden.
You would stop by rain and sun.
Never hesitated.
Always dedicated.
Put yourself last.
We shared a drink from a glass.
You are the light in the rain.
Stand by me through all the pain.
Always went out of your way.
Tried to say thank you every day.
I could always look up to you.
You would sit next to me in school.
The coolest brother I could ever have.
You would make me laugh.
You never complained about my disability.
Good times through creativity.
You stood up for me toward those who made fun of me.
Always patient and unique.
I called you Rain Man.
Because you understand.

8/16

Raining Chaos

No one anchors their mouth.
Vulgar ventures out.
Tongue to slither.
Nothing tame but absurd.
People thrive to destroy.
Someone's reputation.
Never open-minded, only ruined to deploy.
Jump to conclusions.
Spread the drama.
In the middle of chaos.
You never walked in their shoes.
Imperfections out the window.
Never slow to anger.
You have all the answers.
The sky above is never blue.
Cancer bleeding through and through.
The mind racing with envy.
You robbed their identity.

7/5/25

Redemption

Sometimes numb.
Blurred all around.
Sometimes lost.
Life Squandered.
Open up a new door.
Redemption, move forward.
Maybe an unexpected blessing.
Halt, weathervane.
Mistakes to grow.
Deliverance-Rescue
Impossible-Effort
Stay humble, new beginnings.

1/3/25

Remedy Rhythms

Sometimes writer's block
Sunrises at dawn
Sometimes secrets revealed
Render revolver
Rivers soothing recedes
Reckoning subsides
Rain randomly pouring
Sometimes a hole in the sky
Life ripens rosaries
Good deeds to kindness remedy
Rent is paid
Giving is a good day
Better to give than receive
Knowing to reasoning

8/1/25

Rhododendron

Red tree.
Woody growth free.
Red flower.
Ornamental cluster.
Fields of red.
Heavenly run scarlet.
Walk freely through open fields.
Open spaces.
Decorative brood.
Behind dwarf shadows at noon.
Rhododendron.
Monarch transcends.

12/2

Rise Up

Stand for what you believe in
Observe and be obedience
Help your brothers during troubles
The Cross, return home
Walk the narrow road
Wicked ways no more
Surrender, Rise Up
Heaven is limitless
Don't follow ways of the world
Be ready to fly above
Luminous is everywhere
Wait for the trumpets
Out of the old
Into the new
Clothed in white
Taken out of sight

8/11/25

Rolling Stones To Heavenly Skies

Bury the guilt.
Sorrows can heal.
Shadows get behind me.
He knows my name.
I can't ever thank him enough.
The Nails and the Cross.
He alleviated all the pain.
He suffered for everyone knowing.
He walked on water.
There is no other.
Jesus is the only way.
Rolling stones to heavenly skies.
He moves mountains.
He waits for us above the horizon.
Rhythms through poetry.
Rise up, he believes in me.
A letter to the sky.
The wind carries our prayers,
So divine.

6/29/25

Root Of All Evil

Engraved images.
Never enough.
Love of money.
Always greedy.
Root of all evil.
False idols.
Rich and famous.
Collect the paper presidents.
Always want more.
A million-dollar home.
I can do without.
Don't want to be anyone else.
You can be successful.
Don't follow the crowd.
Keep writing poems.
Keep life simple.
Don't carry the world.
No silver nor gold.

10/11

Running Out Of Spaces

Consumed by poetry
Over six years of writing
A phenomenon to reach #1,000 poems
Compassion burning furnace
Solitude through creative writings
Revealeth many short stories
Thirst for knowledge
Running out of blank spaces
Eyes are heavy
Soon the ink will run dry
Chained down to an old rusty desk
Like rain to a desert
Henceforth a whirlwind of ideas
Dwelling upon unwritten literature
Am I a poet?
Do I need validation?
Keep writing in the dark
Breathe in your next poem
With immeasurable weight
Clouds indigo feathered tapestry
I am not Emily Dickinson
Just one more letter
Strive to improve
Poetry is Therapeutic
Running out of empty spaces
Timed against an hourglass
Live just long enough to write 1,000 poems before I die

7/28/25

Salvation

Deliverance from sin.
Life is a whirlwind.
Captive in bondage.
Overwhelmed burdens.
Put your pride aside.
Not through your understanding.
Change of heart.
Fulfillment, endure.
Gain wisdom as you grow.
With discipline, we set an example.
Proclaim redemption.
Yielding to selfishness.
Once a carpenter.
Once a teacher.
He walked among us.
Heavenly skies rolling stones.
He is our savior.

7/14/25

Seed Take Root

Plant goodness.
Up-root abundance.
No complaining.
Just saying.
No limitations.
Up-lifting.
A positive direction.
Miracle beyond words.
Roots toward new beginnings.
Wake up in the morning.
Plant a gift.
No self-doubt.
Seeds of greatness.
Beyond sound.
Plant encouragement.
Soothing waters through the current.
Set a new path.
A hard life won't last.

10/21

Seek Knowledge

People are hungry for spiritual nourishment.
Need rest from all of the chaos.
Your vision is blurry.
With heavy burdens, always worried.
With gossip, always complaining.
Never open-minded.
Castings stones at others.
A path of the unrighteous.
Never open to change.
It has to be always your way.
Separate yourself from the world.
Greedy but unfulfilled.
Only focus on wants and needs.
Never giving. Always receiving.
Blaming someone else.
Never take accountability.
Aggressive and always with anger yelling.
Never slow to anger.
Takes time to mature.
A new road, follow the cross.
Barry, your old ways.
Rise up and be humble.
This is the new me.

6/25/25

Shadows Of The Cross

Walk in faith.
Enemies at my feet.
Carry the cross.
Stand for what you believe in.
Foundation on the rock.
Peace maker.
Travel with sandals.
Courage through the storm.
See past the horizon.
Walk with boldness.
He walks beside me.
When I am weary.
His blood paid it all.
Shadows of the Cross.
Ascended to the sky.
We will meet again one day.

12/20

She Speaks Through Me

December 30th 1830

May 15th 1886

139 years ago

You wrote extraordinaire poetry

Can't fathom, so many

Creative thinking

Creative writing

Cultivating pen in hand

Thoughts racing to the ends of the earth

A small desk to write on

So long ago

I'm right here with you

Massachusetts to Texas

I can only imagine ever meeting you in person

You speak to me through brilliant poetry

How did you even find me?

I'm writing with a learning disability

Maybe one day

Upon velvet skies

Poetry found us beyond the azure horizons

Send me a postcard

Through rhymes and rhythms from heaven

(Emily Dickinson)

8/14/25

Sins Under The Blood

Repent and change your sinful ways.
His suffering lasted three days.
Hinder to anger.
Patience through the winter.
A compass in the right direction.
Don't be discouraged. He
gave us our name.
When we fall away,
A surprising victory unexpected.
Thank him for all of your blessings.
He laid down his life.
Our sins are buried under his blood.
Don't follow the world.
Jesus is the remedy, when we are lost.

7/14/25

Somewhere In Time 1912

It started with a photograph of a young woman.
A love story that should have been.
A story that traveled back in time.
He just wanted her, so divine.
1975 back to 1912.
Obsessed with her into a new realm.
A writer going into the past.
Only if it would last.
One night is all we need.
Plead, come back to me.
A vintage place so long ago.
Ends of the earth to find you.
Standing face to face.
He showed her a penny 1979 mint date.
He lost everything.
Sent forward into the present time.
Love lost from one mistake.
She saw the future, it's too late.
With a radiant smile, she was gone.
A romantic monologue through a song.
Through hypnotism, in time one chance.
Love through an old photograph.

8/29

Sparrows Take Flight

Small silhouette Flying
Shadows sun shining
A humble flight
Today is mine
Capture the moment
With a colorful horizon
Early morning creature
Beautiful sky, here and there
Azure is everywhere
Painted sky, Awe, with white delicate clouds

3/20/25

Spiritual Blindness

Consumed by greed.
Always demanding.
High expectations.
Family dissolving.
A workaholic.
Working yourself to death.
Eyes for another.
Tempted to leave her.
Worship the flesh.
Money is never at rest.
Controlling other people.
Put yourself on a pedestal.
To own the world.
Never enough.
Never content.
Spiritual blindness. Poisoned desires.
Fame and fortune.
Never humble.
Always hungry for more.
To gain the world.
To sell your soul.
Idolize only yourself.
Putting God last.
Materialistic.
Family on the back burner. Kids never see you.
Money is the only priority.

Spiritual blindness.
Constant rage.
What cost to throw it all away.

7/10/25

Spiritual Words

Redeemed, saved from sin.
Being merciful on his behalf.
Salvation, through deliverance.
Covenants, an agreement to keep his law.
The ten commandments.
To be faithful under the sun.
Merciful, showing compassion.
Faith, trust and belief.
Justification, humankind not accountable, free of penalty.
Grace, elegance and beauty.
Humble, down to earth, giving not receiving.

6/25/25

Standing On The Promise

I'm in error.
Beyond burdens.
Carry the weight.
Quiet, will be.
Impatient, I've always been.
Must I interrupt?
What if?
Need a blessing?
Under pressure always.
Be open-minded.
Turn the pages.
New chapter, never too late.
A promise.
Every day is a gift.
He thought of you.
Even before you were born.

Jeremiah 1:5

10/20

Stretches For Miles

Flowers in the garden.
Melodies for miles.
At the cross with many smiles.
Illustrations painted beautiful colors.
Through him, we are delivered.
A spiritual awakening.
Past the horizon is a mystery.
Forgiveness is purity.
Arms stretch for miles.
Sunsets into tomorrow.
Absent from dark.
The end of the storm remains the cross.
Prayers echo.
Autumn to ambers.
With Jesus, we need no other.
Rain for 1,000 years.

7/13/25

Sweet Sound

Music that moves you
Song from a piano
No words needed
Use your imagination
Be still
Feel the wind
Music takes you places
With harmony, through empty spaces
Rhyme through poetry
Write your own journey
Face the sun
Beautiful through song
You raise me up
Sweetest sound
An old soul
Just wanted to say thank you
Clouds above us
So meaningful
Don't let go
Hold on to the sun

3/17/25

Swinging From A Tire

The good old days.
So carefree.
Swinging from a tire.
Living in the country, no other.
Two people with a child.
Always a smile.
Winds carry memories.
Afternoon tea.
These were the days.
Now she is 20.
I miss both of you.
Just wanted to say thank you.
Little girl growing up.
Swinging from a tree.
Drive back once more.
Parents rest under.
Drive through the open sky.
Another poem in the light.

12/31

Thanks Mom

A hard life.
Sun Blind.
Tough street.
Stand on my own two feet.
Thanks for everything you do.
Can't live without you.
Doing my best.
Sorry I'm a mess.
You made me a hot plate.
You worked so late.
Greatest mom.
Can never thank you enough.
Just trying to give back.
You were there when I was bad.
I ran away.
Open arms someday.
Just a phone call away. I just wanted to say.

11/24

Thanksgiving

Detailed-Kitchen Table
Food-All Around
Bloated-After Ward
Family-Gathering
Football & Turkey
Orange-Leaves
Fall-Season
Autumn-Weather
Pumpkin Pie & Coffee
Time Off-Away
Kick Back-Relax
Second Plate-All The fixings
Thanksgiving-A Blessing
Serve-Hot Plate For Others
Those In Need-Give To The
Apple Cider-Humble Provider
Great Food-New Memories Every Year
Happy Thanksgiving

10/14

The Boat

Where do you stand in your life?
How do you face tomorrow in flight?
What about the 12 men who were worried in the storm?
Believe and be calm like before.
Knowing that you have lost your way.
Tomorrow brings a brighter day.
On the boat you feared the night.
As the winds blew, yield to the rain that's in sight.
Carry the lamp that shows the way.
Surpass the raging waters, stand brave.
You have forgotten how much he cares.
Through his voice, nothing else compares.
Sometimes we rush into thorns and worry.
We don't ask for help in pride, our vision is blurry.
The storm on the boat has subsided.
Through him, sail on the water into the light.
Our lives are short just like the passing wind.
The stripes he carried were in red.
Drift downstream under a colorful sky.
Be open-minded and never say goodbye.
Walk on the narrow road.
He will find you no matter how far he has to go.
Along the way he has always been a friend. One day above, we will meet again.

Luke 8:24

The Cross

Before I was even born,
In blood, you were torn.
The road you walked alone was hard to follow.
You showed me there is no other way but a narrow road.
At the beginning you were a carpenter.
You took me by the hand knowing this will last forever.
You would stand tall toward the sun.
At the door you sent an invitation.
No matter how far I have fallen,
With the sacrifice you made, you comfort me with devotion.
You carried the weight of the world.
After the rock was moved, you were raised with light from the burial.
How painful it was with a crown of thorns.
You held me close with open arms.
At The Cross, it changed my life.
The blood given was the greatest sacrifice.
One day we will meet again.
Through a parable, it will be green grass in the garden.
To be in your presents is a blessing.
The gift that saved us is overwhelming.
I don't even deserve a second chance.
Through him and repentance he is the first and last.
Even though I'm drowning in the cold, You
walked beside me and saved me from below.
In the sky with many colors you knew my name.

You believed in me, and you broke the chain.
No more will I be held down in sin.
By your grace I am not forsaken.
Through the hammer and nail, you never hesitated.
The love you gave us will never fade.

4/8/23

The Falling Away

An angel that rebelled.
Had it all but failed.
Envy of the most high.
The king of all lies.
Rules over a lawless society.
Don't follow his ways.
Cancer bleeding in the world.
It lives in the dark.
The Falling Away is here.
Watching from everywhere.
Want no part of it.
Hold on to the cross.
Fallen to the pet of death.
Darkness upon us.
Behind the curtain is a disguise.
Angel to demon flies.
Stand by the sword.
Carry the lamp in the dark.
Know where you belong.
In the sky, not far.

10/22

The Good Samaritan

A man half dead on the side of the road.
Two men walked by, they didn't want to be bothered.
Soon a stranger stopped to help.
Truly thankful, he was overwhelmed.
Brought the man into town.
Give without asking for anything in return.
A good man went out of his way.
Share a story through testimony.
A good Samaritan is hard to find.
Are you that person or blind?
Help is always needed.
Make good choices.
Be the lamp in the dark.
Ask and I won't be far.
The world is so consumed.
Take only for themselves.
Every man for himself.
Always busy is a selfish world.
Be grateful.
Stay humble.
Don't complain about your problems.
Don't worry about tomorrow.
Just take one day at a time.
Because time flies by.

Luke 10:25-37

8/2

The Last Crumb

I saw some birds fighting over some bread.

Everyone fights each other until they're dead.

The birds were after the last thing to eat.

The whole world is blind, they cannot see.

A civil war to prove someone wrong.

People being respectful are long gone.

What happened to everyone?

Just to be a good samaritan to someone.

To fight for the last crumb that's on the ground.

Each man for himself just to drown.

How can you reach out to a lost generation?

The world bleeds through separation.

Would you give your last piece of bread to a stranger?

Giving to someone would be your last waver. Be a leader and not a follower.

If you don't put in the work then don't bother.

Find your own way through forgiveness.

Standing humble in lightness.

Speak no lies to your brothers.

Hold up the lantern for others.

We find purpose through prosperity.

To give your best from clarity.

Take a stand against the oppressors. Give back all that you are.

9/18

The Narrow Road

Walk the narrow road.
Keep life simple on your own.
Take time out to enjoy life.
Stay humble in delight.
A footpath on the sand.
In the dark, hold up the lamp.
Help others in need.
Walk through faithfully.
Don't be a part of this world.
With guidance, don't worry about tomorrow.
Don't take life for granted.
Stay focused through ambition.
The river flows through us.
Be grateful, for it is just.
Valuables are meaningless in our lives.
You can't take them with you when you die.
We all carry many burdens. Be open-minded and listen. Leave it all at the cross.
Seek all those who are lost.
Don't complain about your troubles.
He understands through sorrow.
Be at peace in your life.
He waits for us in the sky.

6/13

Matthew 7:13

The Other Side Of Me

Always focused and sincere
Who am I through a blemish storm?
Calm, won't budge
The other side of me
Upmost surreal with creativity
A simple loner
Mind always bending through silent whispers
Stillness with confidence
Don't reveal too much
A writer at dark eternal dusk
Ink bleeds off the pages
Just another paper cut
I don't have to wear a haunted mask
I've always been honest
Just an old man who writes therapeutic poems
I'm not much for a sense of humor
Always a deep thinker
A poet I've become
Work in hand never done
Free thinkers on paper
Mind traveling music makers
Just an old soul
Down to earth

8/18/25

The Piano

You have my undivided attention.
In a blue sky, it's with devotion. With
grace, you speak kind words to me, Past
the Horizon, only you can see. What lies
ahead, when you turn the page To meet
someone new across the bay. I see you
for the first time is like, Seeing heaven in the sky.
Whatever path we may take, Every
day will be meaningful to save.
These are our memories to begin,
Under the sunset, only you understand.
The sound of a piano is you, It is
meant to be, to hold you soon.
Thank you for all the sacrifices you've made,
You are my equal every day.
When you express yourself in a song,
I truly know where I belong.
I don't want this to be too short, Maybe
one day, you will be at my door.
These words I only give to you, Are like the
songs you play that are so beautiful.
Each note I hear is like rain from above, You
have lifted up these burdens, with love. Even
though you may be far,
I know you are playing a song like Sapphire.

The Poem I Left Behind.

To a hazed day.
Rose petals by your feet.
Your eyes are amber in the light.
Touch so divine.
The wind catches the pages.
Dreaming mystery, to fade.
Write you another letter.
Looking at the fall colors.
Speechless.
In your presents.
Just looking out the window.
There will be no other.
The poem I left behind.
Candles burn bright, you are mine.
Where do we go from here?
You've always been sincere.
Even if the roses fade.
I'm thankful to be with you every day.

10/10

The Ten Commandments

You shall have no other gods before me.

You shall not make for yourself any graven images.

You shall not take the name of the Lord In vain.

Remember the Sabbath day to keep it holy.

Honor your father and mother. You shall not kill.

You shall not commit adultery.

You shall not steal.

You shall not bear false witness.

You shall not covet.

I am just a messenger.

Know right from wrong.

We are all sinners.

I'm not here to cast out stones. I've always been spiritual.
There is no shame, In his name.

Walk the narrow road.

Don't follow the crowd.

When you're in the storm.

Trust in him.

He will walk beside you.

He gave us our name.

He died on the cross for you and me.

Through him, is the only way.

We will meet again one day.

Our lives on earth are short.

We are preparing for something more.
We are brothers.
Welcome home in many colors.

7/11/25

<u>Poem #900</u>

The Tower Of Babel

A covenant with descendants.
Another generation entered.
With one language, they understood.
They began to build towards the Heavens.
With brick and mortar.
Build a city tower.
With arrogant to idolize themselves.
A building to reach their own gods.
Men were scattered abroad.
With confusion, became The Tower Of Babel.
No one could communicate.
Hard labor to build selfishness to the skies.
Everyone just walked away dismayed.

6/29/25

The Weather Is Calm

A cup of tea
A delightful morning
No worries
Vibrant and soothing
Ginger and spice
Turn the page
The weather is calm
Capture the moment
Nothing is distorted
Peace of mind
Sometimes daydreaming
Spiritual nourishment
Calming environment
Perfect ingredients
Just pondering
Alternate reality
Walking into a new season
With an ironically view

6/21/25

Therapeutic

Therapeutic, is soothing.
Maybe some hot tea.
Something meaningful to everyone.
Hobbies and talents.
Your favorite pastime.
For me, it's writing poetry.
Sounds from a piano in the background.
Time away from work.
What is your therapeutic recipe?
It could be anything pleasing.
Spending time with someone.
Kicking back being a couch potato.
Whatever it may be.
A therapeutic moment
heavenly.

6/9/25

Thief In The Night

I will rain in the clouds.
My return will be beyond sound.
I will be a thief in the night.
I will take with authority what is mine.
Believe in me for I am the beginning and the end.
I reach out my hand to you as a friend.
Don't be afraid of the dark.
One day I will be knocking at your door.
For I am the light and the way.
There will be false prophets pretending to take my place.
Walk the narrow road, and don't stray too far.
Hold up the candle like a star.
Trust in me always.
I have a home for you above far away.
You have always been a part of me.
I will take your place when you are suffering.
I hold you up like you are my son.
I am proud of you for what you have done.
You are down-to-earth and humble.
You would put yourself last and help others when they stumble.
You're everything to me.
I suffered on the cross because you believed.
In the darkest days I will return.
Everything and everyone against me will burn.
The blood I shed for you is all you need.
Through me you can be free.

10/22/23

2 Peter 3:10

215

Urban Spaces

The world is getting smaller.
People become dwellers.
A new life of solo living.
A single life of well-being.
Do we all have anxiety?
Through loneliness especially.
Maybe we have lost trust in each other.
Walk on by, don't even bother.
Some live in urban spaces.
Pass on by many faces.
We become too independent.
Individual living to the limit.
No social life.
Just breathe to get by.
We lost the human touch.
With no one to love.
We can't see in the fog.
A lonely life is now common.
Where did everyone go?
A generation hiding behind their cell phones.
What happened to you and me?
Everything was wonderful in the blue sky.
Maybe, will have a chance through the sunlight?
I would hold you close at night.
I guess we are now all solitude.
Just a lifetime to wake up next to you.

6/11

Value Every Minute

Document your life
Leave it all behind
I've become a deep thinker
Always a loner
Mind always racing
Hard to fall asleep
Always behind with my work
Sometimes end up with writer's block
Need more coffee
I'm running out of time
Keep on writing
Before the ink runs dry
My Philosophy
Read in between the lines
Through poetry
There is no other way
Life is fading
Value every minute
Through body
language
Completely focused
We are writers

4/16/25

Walk Beside Me

My burdens are heavy.
The gray is catching up with me.
I'm running out of time.
My body is dying.
Buried in many tribulations.
Walk beside me in the storm.
You show compassion when I'm out of patience.
Help me with guidance.
Aches and pains echo.
Suffer into tomorrow.
Drown in a broken world.
Walk the narrow road.
Help me when I'm lost.
Show me the way past the horizon.
Carry my burdens.
You gave me my name.
Amen.

2/6/25

Walk On Water

Walk on water
I surrender all
Trust in me
To man, save the
For I am the way
Through turmoil, I will stay
I will walk with you in the storm
I knew you even before you were even born
I knocked at your door
For the water is clear
There is no other way
Hold on to the truth
Grow through principle
This life I give you
I will see you again in the clouds
I have a place for you
Remember me always
I gave you your name

4/13/25

Walk With Me On The Clouds

Where have you been?
So much time lost
You disappeared
You're so far away
Smiles left behind
Just pondering
Still searching
The wind scatters our ashes
Together with the time we have left
Melody with sound
Uneven paths are found
Standing on the bridge
New beginnings ahead
Walk with me on the clouds
I found you at last

3/22/25

We Are Writers

No one understands us.
Ink to blood.
Empty pages.
Mind always racing.
Thyself obscure.
Boundless pen
traveler. Melody
through smoke.
Sober storyteller.
Dark writer.
Candles radiant burn.
Mechanical thinker.
Obsessive writing disorder.
Lonely for a reason.
Disconnected through seasons.
Type away open fields.
We are writers. Poets on fire.

11/7

What Is Eternity?

Little bread
Little crumbs
Little trust
Make your own way
Become dust one day
For now, just be you
Down to earth
Don't need much
Little sophisticated
Little trivial
Little mysteries
Wild at times
Write your own chapter, somewhat revealing
My mind is a little crowded
Another poem to write
Soon evening night
Solitude I shall be
What is Eternity?
Your own personal journey

7/1/25

When I'm Gone

Hold all of my poems
When I'm gone
Not for too long
Just the two of us
A beautiful melody song
I haven't' forgotten
Memories through reflections
Walking hand in hand
You are the only one
Smiles I'll hold on to
You were there when I needed someone the most
Velvet skies hold us close
No one could ever replace you
I give you one last rose
Patient, I shall be
You're so unique
In your Victorian ways
Walk the long mile
I'm sorry for the words I should have said
No sorrows ahead
A new chapter in the clouds
Heaven is all around
Colorful dreams
At the gates, I'll be waiting

3/26/25

When Jesus Was Baptized

A voice calling from the wilderness.
To make a straight path for him.

A walk to the Jordan River.
Baptized for everyone to see through the clouds.

Sink under water to repentance.
Rise through the holy spirit, become new.

Be fulfilled by righteousness.
Go your own way on the narrow road.

Keep me from temptation.
Speak the good news.

Walk on the path with obedience.
Show me the way.

As doves are alighting,
A voice from Heaven said,
This is my son whom I love, with him I am well pleased

7/14/25

When We Lose Our Way

A place we call home
A long journey alone
Astray off course
Guidance on a new road
Find your way back
Poor choices along the way
Only blame myself
Learn to grow
I still have time to change
Put the past behind
Put the wrong things right
Someone's watching from above
Let this be our prayer
Watch us where we go
The road back home
Guide us through the sky
Leave our troubles behind

4/28/25

Winding Roads

You never know what's around the corner
Be alert
Know your
surroundings
Survive toward longevity
Be sharp-minded
Grow by learning
Be strategic
Put life on cruise control
Be slow to anger
You have the potential
It's OK to slow down
Don't worry about everyone else
Be your own man
Winding roads takes you somewhere new
Smooth roads, be cool
No worries
Be a mystery
Life is short
Enjoy every minute
Don't take life for granted
You don't always have to have the last word
I feel like we're growing old faster
Take time out to smell the roses
Don't follow the crowd
Fly like an eagle

4/23/25

Worldly Things

Materialistic

Manipulation

Temptations

Slaves to money

Power Hungry

Everything the eye can see

Your wants and needs Lust for another

Outside your marriage

Worth the risk

Flesh is for the taking

With no spiritual direction

No discipline

No self-control

A high roller

Money spent like no day tomorrow

No care for others

Walk on by past the poor

Alter ego

Only warship yourself

You have all the answers

Always a cheater

You will be lonely in the end

6/25/25

Wrap Your Arms Around The Earth

Destruction around the world.
Mother Nature at work.
Storms on the rise.
Buildings on fire.
Wiped off the map.
Submerged and trapped.
Need a heavenly blessing.
World crisis at the brink.
A hard life after the flood.
Bridges collapse, going under.
Survive After the storm.
Many homes are gone.
Wrap your arms around the earth.
With so many impacted areas.
Reach out for those in need.
Water subsiding.
All overwhelming.
Another hurricane.
Just heartbreaking.
Nothing will be the same.

10/1

Your Eyes Move Me

Touch a smile.
With you for the long mile.
Humble in your path.
Walk hand in hand.
White as Ivory.
(Cloths) Your eyes
move me.
You said yes, no matter how hard my life has been.
You have my undivided attention.
Never take you for granted.
You've looked past my imperfections.

10/20